Franklin D. Roosevelt

Franklin D. Roosevelt

Barbara Silberdick Feinberg

AMERICA'S 32ND PRESIDENT

Children's Press®
A Division of Scholastic Inc.
New York / Toronto / London / Auckland / Sydney
Mexico City / New Delhi / Hong Kong
Danbury, Connecticut

Library of Congress Cataloging-in-Publication Data

Feinberg, Barbara Silberdick.
      Franklin D. Roosevelt / Barbara Silberdick Feinberg.
         p. cm. — (Encyclopedia of presidents. Second series)
   Includes bibliographical references and index.
    Audience: Grades 7–8.
    ISBN 0-516-22970-2
      1. Roosevelt, Franklin D. (Franklin Delano), 1882–1945—Juvenile literature.
   2. Presidents—United States—Biography—Juvenile literature. I. Title. II.
   Encyclopedia of presidents (2003)
   E807.F348 2005
   973.917'092—dc22   2004018927

Contents

Chapter 1

An Extraordinary President

Franklin Delano Roosevelt was the 32nd president of the United States. He was one of the most extraordinary figures in American history, gaining election to the office four times (no other president was elected more than twice) and serving more than 12 years. Long before his election, Roosevelt had been disabled by disease. His legs were paralyzed, and he could not walk, getting around in a wheelchair. When he became president in 1933, the nation was paralyzed by a disastrous economic collapse (later known as the Great Depression). Roosevelt's optimistic spirit brought hope to millions who were unemployed, and his decisive actions helped get the nation's economy moving again.

Roosevelt might have served only two terms as president, but by the end of his second term in 1940, the world was engulfed by war.

President Roosevelt brought a new sense of hope to Americans as they struggled through the Great Depression in the 1930s.

Much of Europe was occupied by the armies of Nazi Germany, and Asia was threatened by Japanese aggression. It appeared that the United States might soon be involved in the fighting. Voters trusted Roosevelt to lead them through another great crisis and elected him to a third term. The United States entered the war in 1941, and Roosevelt worked with other Allied leaders, helping determine the course of the war and making plans for the postwar world.

As World War II reached a climax late in 1944, voters elected Roosevelt to a fourth term. His health was failing, however, and he died in April 1945, four months before World War II ended in victory over both Germany and Japan. Weeks after his death, his dream of a more peaceful world came closer to realization when delegates from many countries established the United Nations.

Childhood

Franklin Delano Roosevelt was born on January 30, 1882, the only child of James Roosevelt and Sara Delano Roosevelt. Both of his parents came from prominent New York families. The Roosevelts were descended from the early Dutch settlers. The first Roosevelt arrived in 1649 and began a long line of successful merchants. The Delano family traced its origin to a passenger on the *Fortune*, a ship that arrived at Plymouth in 1621, just a year after the *Mayflower*. Most of the Delanos were shipowners and international merchants. Sara even lived in China with her family for three years when she was a child.

In 1880, James Roosevelt was a 52-year-old widower with an adult son. He met and married 25-year-old Sara Delano. The new couple lived on the Roosevelt estate in Hyde Park, New York, about 75 miles (120 kilometers) north of New York City. James was a country gentleman who managed investments and properties he had inherited. Sara enjoyed looking after him and later their baby son, who was named after her uncle, Franklin Delano.

Sara was a very devoted and protective mother. She kept Franklin in long curls past babyhood. She also made him wear kilts—which he thought of as skirts—until he objected at age eight. Sara set up a schedule for Franklin's daily activities, deciding when he should study, play, bathe, and eat. Franklin rarely refused his mother's orders, but early in life he learned how to get his own way by charming her rather than resorting to tantrums or tears. He often used charm to get his way for the rest of his life.

Franklin's parents helped shape his lifelong interests. Sara encouraged him to collect stamps. On afternoon rides with James Roosevelt around the estate, Franklin learned to care about land and trees. His father also taught him to sled, fish, iceboat, and swim. James Roosevelt may also have passed along his support for the Democratic party. When Franklin was only five, his father took him to the

Left, Franklin at 18 months with his father, James Roosevelt. Right, he poses at 11 years old with his mother, Sara Delano Roosevelt.

White House to visit Democratic president Grover Cleveland. Cleveland patted the little boy on the head and said, "My little man, I am making a strange wish for you. It is that you may never be president of the United States."

The Roosevelts often traveled in their private railroad car to visit relatives or to reach their summer house on the Canadian island of Campobello, off the coast of Maine. There Franklin came to love the sea and sailing ships. When he was 14, he learned to sail *Half Moon*, the family yacht. The family also traveled often to Europe. Franklin had made nine visits there before he was 18.

Franklin received his early schooling from a series of governesses, who taught him penmanship, arithmetic, Latin, French, and German under Sara's supervision. Most of the time, he was surrounded by adults rather than children. He played with his cousins or the children of Hyde Park workers only occasionally.

Boarding School Student

When he was 14, Franklin was enrolled at the Groton School, in Groton, Massachusetts, about 50 miles (80 km) outside Boston. At home he had been the center of attention with doting parents and a household staff to attend to his needs. Now he was just one of 110 boys. He occupied a tiny room with a curtain for a door and was responsible for keeping it tidy.

Most boys began studying at Groton when they were 12. When Franklin arrived, the boys his age had already formed friendships, and it was hard for a new boy to break in. He must have been lonely during his early weeks, but in his letters home, he described himself as "fine," keeping his private feelings to himself. Keeping his thoughts to himself became a lifelong habit.

Gradually Franklin began to make friends. He sang in the choir, took part in plays, and learned to debate. The other boys were from backgrounds similar to his, so he soon fit in and made some friendships that lasted for

Endicott Peabody's Groton

Endicott Peabody (1857–1944), an Episcopal minister, began Groton in 1884. Peabody hoped to develop character as well as intelligence in his well-to-do students, so he required the boys to attend religious services, to participate in team sports, and to live plainly. The students followed a strict daily routine, ending each evening when they each shook hands with Rector and Mrs. Peabody before preparing for bed.

Peabody stressed his students' responsibility to become leaders and look out for those less fortunate than themselves. "If some Groton boys do not enter political life and do something for our land," he once said, "it won't be because they have not been urged." Roosevelt admired Rector Peabody. Later he would ask Peabody to perform his wedding ceremony and to conduct private services in the White House before his inaugurations.

☆ ☆ ☆

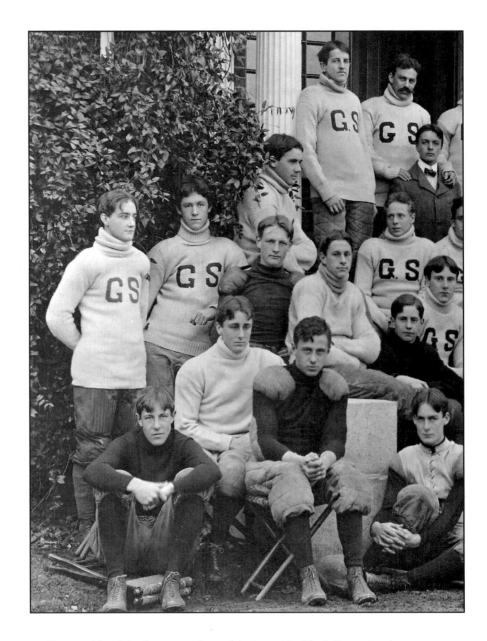

Franklin (second from left in front row) with part of the Groton School football team. Since he was not a member of the varsity and did not receive a letter, he wore a plain white sweater.

decades. He was no success at sports, though, struggling to make the fourth-string football team.

During Franklin's years at Groton, he first began to appreciate his distant cousin, Theodore Roosevelt. (Their great-grandfathers were brothers.) Theodore, 23 years older, had been a prominent Republican in New York City and was now assistant secretary of the navy in Washington. Franklin became determined to follow his cousin's footsteps into politics.

By the time Franklin graduated from Groton in 1900, he had brought his grades up from a C to about a B average, and he had won awards for being on time and for Latin studies. He had also completed a year of college-level work. The Reverend Peabody described him as "a quiet, satisfactory boy of more than ordinary intelligence."

Harvard Man

In 1900, Franklin entered Harvard College. Like other boys from wealthy families, he rented rooms in a fashionable neighborhood and soon got caught up in the social whirl of dances and parties. He wrote home, "My dress suit looked like a dream and was much admired." However, some young women called him a "feather duster" behind his back because he seemed so shallow.

During Franklin's first year at Harvard, his father died. His mother moved to Boston to be near him. He visited her often but still took part in school activities, becoming secretary of the Freshman Glee Club and writing for the Harvard newspaper, the *Crimson*. By this time, his cousin Theodore had been elected vice president of the United States. Franklin got an interview with him and reported the news that Theodore would soon visit the campus. Later that year, when President William McKinley died, Theodore Roosevelt became president.

As a student, Franklin received mostly Cs. He later suggested that classroom learning could be of doubtful value. "I took economics courses in college for four years," he said when he was president, "and everything I was taught was wrong." He completed his requirements for a Harvard degree in three years, but stayed for a fourth year to serve as president (editor in chief) of the *Crimson*. He wrote some stirring editorials (one demanded more fire escapes in dormitories), but most were about sports and other light topics. He was a great supporter of the Harvard football team.

Husband

During his last two years at Harvard, Franklin had an interest beyond classes and college activities. He was courting Eleanor Roosevelt, his fifth cousin. He first met Eleanor on family occasions when they were children. She was three years younger than he and was the daughter of Theodore Roosevelt's brother Elliott. Both of her parents died before she was ten, and she was raised by her strict grandmother. As a girl, Eleanor had been tall, shy, and awkward. When she was 14, her grandmother sent her to study at Allenswood, an exclusive boarding school in Britain. When Franklin met her again in 1902, she was not quite 18, and her years in Britain had given her a new sense of confidence and charm.

Eleanor Roosevelt in 1902.

During the next year, Franklin and Eleanor met secretly and wrote to each other often. They were seen together during a dinner in Theodore Roosevelt's White House in December 1902. Franklin came down from Harvard to visit her in New York City, and in January 1903, she attended his 21st birthday party.

Eleanor wrote later that she fell in love with Franklin because he shared her interest in books. Later in life, Franklin said that he fell in love with her because she had a trait "every member of the Roosevelt family seems always to have had, a deep and abiding interest in everything and everyone." Franklin proposed marriage to Eleanor in the fall of 1903, and she agreed.

"I am the happiest man just now in the world," he told his mother about his engagement to Eleanor. "And for you, dear Mummy, you know that nothing can ever change what we have always been & and will always be to each other—only now you have two children to love & to love you."

Sara Roosevelt was shocked to learn of her son's planned marriage. Hoping to break up the relationship, she insisted that the couple keep their engagement secret for a full year. They obeyed, but as soon as the year was up, they announced their intention to marry. That same month, Franklin cast his first vote for president, forsaking the Democratic candidate to vote for his cousin (and Eleanor's uncle) Theodore Roosevelt.

Franklin and Eleanor were married in New York City on March 17, 1905. Endicott Peabody presided at the ceremony, and President Roosevelt gave the bride away. The president congratulated

Eleanor and Franklin Roosevelt during their honeymoon in 1905.

Franklin for "keeping the name in the family." After the ceremony, the guests flocked to meet the president, almost ignoring the newlyweds. By this time, Franklin was a student at the Columbia University School of Law in New York. He and Eleanor put off their honeymoon until the end of the school term. Then they spent their summer in Europe.

Chapter 2

Family Matters

In the fall of 1905, the newlyweds returned to New York City, and Franklin continued his law studies. They lived in an apartment that had been chosen and furnished by Sara. She took charge of the couple's daily lives, choosing their servants and the furnishings for their home. When Eleanor saw some of the furniture her mother-in-law had selected, she burst into tears. Franklin disliked arguments, so Eleanor had to submit meekly to Sara's wishes.

She was pregnant by this time. Anna Roosevelt was born in 1906, and in the next ten years, Eleanor gave birth to five sons, one of whom died in infancy.

In 1907 Franklin passed the New York State bar examination, qualifying him to practice law in the state. He gave up further law study and went to work as a clerk for the law firm of Carter, Ledyard

& Milburn. The following year, Sara gave the young family a handsome town house in a fashionable New York City neighborhood. The catch was that Sara took up residence in the town house next door and arranged for passageways between the two houses on each floor. Sara decided how the growing children would be raised and competed with Eleanor for their love.

State Senator

In 1910, Roosevelt ran for the New York State Senate from the upstate area around Hyde Park. He traveled with other local candidates who taught him how to run for office. For example, he learned to create a personal tie to his audience by saying something about the local areas. Speaking from the back of a red open-air car, he declared himself a reform Democrat and attacked the corrupt *bosses* in both parties. Bosses controlled powerful political organizations that awarded government contracts and other favors in exchange for money or votes. Franklin often mentioned his Uncle Theodore, who had retired as U. S. president the year before. On election day, Franklin defeated his Republican opponent 15,708 to 14,568.

Franklin and Eleanor moved to Albany, the state capital, and rented a large house. Now for the first time, Eleanor could manage her own household without competition from her mother-in-law. She made it a place where Franklin

Franklin Roosevelt makes a campaign speech during his first run for office in 1910.

could meet with fellow legislators to plan political strategy. The reformers were opposing Charles F. Murphy of New York City, the most powerful Democrat in the state. At the time, U.S. senators were elected by state legislatures, and Boss Murphy supported one of his associates, "Blue-Eyed Billy" Sheehan, to represent the state in the Senate.

As a reformer, Roosevelt spoke out fearlessly against Murphy and his organization, known as Tammany Hall. "Murphy and his kind must, like the noxious weed, be plucked out, root and branch," he thundered. The reformers refused to vote for Sheehan's nomination for the Senate. Tammany finally agreed to drop its demand for Sheehan's nomination, and the reformers agreed to vote for Judge James A. O'Gorman, another Tammany member. Roosevelt considered this a victory in his first skirmish with the New York City bosses.

In 1912 Roosevelt joined other Democratic reformers in supporting New Jersey governor Woodrow Wilson for president. Wilson was a leading Democrat in the Progressive movement, which urged increased government action to make life better for American citizens. They wanted the government to support conservation, provide cheap electric power, inspect food and drugs for purity, and improve the health and safety of workingmen.

The Democrats of Tammany Hall opposed the Progressives and made sure that they were not chosen as delegates to the Democratic National Convention, which would nominate the party's presidential candidate. The Progressives went to the convention anyway but could not vote during the balloting. Roosevelt led a long floor demonstration for Wilson, who eventually won the presidential nomination on the 46th ballot. In November, Wilson became the first Democrat in 20 years to be elected president.

Franklin Roosevelt was also on the ballot to gain re-election to the state senate. Early in the campaign season, however, he came down with typhoid fever and was bedridden. He engaged Albany reporter Louis Howe to direct his campaign. Howe organized Roosevelt clubs, toured in Franklin's red car, bought newspaper advertising, and sent out mailings in the candidate's name. Roosevelt won by 1,600 votes, and Louis Howe became a permanent member of his inner circle.

Assistant Secretary of the Navy ───────

In April 1913, Roosevelt's career took a new direction. In recognition of his stature as a prominent young Democrat, President Wilson appointed him assistant secretary of the navy. The position appealed to Roosevelt's lifelong love of the sea and to his interest in military and naval history. It was also a promising stepping-stone to higher office. His cousin Theodore Roosevelt had served in the same post. Roosevelt resigned from the state senate and moved his family to Washington, D.C. He brought Louis Howe to Washington to serve as his assistant.

Roosevelt worked under Secretary of the Navy Josephus Daniels, a leading North Carolina Democrat. As assistant secretary, Roosevelt was responsible for operation of U.S. navy yards, negotiating labor contracts with civilian workers, and purchasing naval supplies. After war broke out in Europe in 1914, Roosevelt was an outspoken supporter of building a stronger navy. "We must create a navy not only to protect our shores and our possessions," he said, "but our merchant ships in time of war, no matter where they may go." Josephus Daniels and many other Democrats were strongly against American involvement in the war (which was later known as World War I). They believed that the United States should remain strictly *neutral*, showing special favor to neither side in the war.

Roosevelt, like President Wilson, believed that the United States should support the Allied powers, including Britain and

Fast Facts
WORLD WAR I

Who: The Central powers (including Germany and Austria-Hungary) against the Allied powers (including Great Britain, France, Russia, and later the U.S.)

When: August 1914 to November 1918

Where: Major battles in Belgium and northern France; along the German-Russian border; along the Austrian-Italian border, and in the Middle East

Why: Long-simmering rivalries between nations were ignited by the assassination of an heir to the Austro-Hungarian throne in June 1914; the U.S. declared war in April 1917 after Germany announced unrestricted submarine warfare in Allied waters.

Outcome: The retreating German army requested an armistice (cease-fire) in November 1918. The Treaty of Versailles, signed in June 1919, reduced the size of Germany and broke up Austria-Hungary, and established the League of Nations, a world organization to settle international disputes.

Roosevelt (far right) appears in Washington with the leaders of the national Democratic party, including President Woodrow Wilson (holding a paper) and William Jennings Bryan (in white suit), who was the Democratic candidate for president three times.

France. When the German navy began attacking U.S. ships carrying food and supplies to Britain, President Wilson wanted to arm U.S. merchant ships but was afraid that Congress would not approve such action. Roosevelt found an old law that Wilson could use to arm the ships without asking for congressional approval. He worried about seeming to favor the Allies in public, however. "I just know I shall do some awful unneutral thing before I get through," he wrote to Eleanor.

Roosevelt reviews U.S. Navy troops in France in 1918, during World War I.

After repeated submarine attacks on U.S. ships, the United States finally entered the war on the side of the Allies in April 1917. Roosevelt helped speed up construction of naval training centers. He pushed through labor contracts and was involved in plans to lay mines in the North Sea against German submarines. During an official visit to Europe in 1918, he got to the front where he was under enemy fire. After the war, he returned to Europe to help dispose of naval property.

Crisis and Defeat

When Roosevelt returned home from France, he was ill, so Eleanor unpacked his bags. She came across a packet of love letters to Franklin from Lucy Mercer, a beautiful young woman who had served as Eleanor's social secretary. Eleanor offered to divorce Franklin, but he declined. He knew that a divorce would shame the family and deeply hurt their children. It would also end any hope he had of gaining elective office at a time when divorces were rare and considered scandalous. Franklin promised that he would never see Lucy again (a promise he did not keep). Eleanor continued to work closely with Franklin on his political career, but she also developed a new sense of independence.

At the 1920 Democratic convention, the party nominated James M. Cox, an Ohio newspaper publisher, to run for president. Franklin Roosevelt won the nomination for vice president. Public sentiment was running against the Democrats, but

A 1920 campaign poster for presidential candidate James M. Cox and vice-presidential candidate Franklin D. Roosevelt. They lost the election to Republicans Warren Harding and Calvin Coolidge.

Roosevelt threw himself into the campaign. In a single two-day stay in the state of Washington, for example, he gave 26 speeches. He met and chatted with dozens of Democratic leaders during his campaign jaunts. On election day, Cox and Roosevelt were defeated by Republicans Warren Harding and Calvin Coolidge by a landslide vote. Despite the lost, Roosevelt had made many new friends who would help him in future campaigns.

The election of a Republican president also meant that Roosevelt would lose his post as assistant secretary of the navy, but he remained cheerful. "Curiously enough, I do not feel in the least bit downhearted," he wrote to a friend.

Chapter 3

Disaster

The Roosevelts returned to New York after nearly eight years in Washington. Franklin became vice president of the Fidelity and Deposit Company and took up the practice of law once again.

That summer the family took a long vacation at the Roosevelt estate on Campobello Island. Roosevelt still loved the seaside house and enjoyed sailing, hiking, and swimming. On August 10, 1921, he came back to the house after a vigorous swim. He later remembered, "I didn't feel the usual reaction, the glow I'd expected. When I reached the house the mail was in, with several newspapers I hadn't seen. I sat reading for a while, too tired even to dress. I'd never felt quite that way before."

He began to complain of a chill and went straight to bed without supper. The next morning, he recalled, "When I swung out of bed my left leg lagged, but I managed to move about and to shave. . . . Presently [the left leg] refused to work, and then the other." He was running a high fever.

Eleanor sent the children off on a camping trip so she could care for Franklin. The day after that he was no longer able to stand, and his legs were painful to the touch. At 39 years old, Franklin had been struck down by *poliomyelitis*, or polio, a contagious disease that seems at first like a bad case of the flu, but can cause permanent damage to nerves and paralyze arms, legs, or lungs, preventing them from functioning. As Franklin's legs became paralyzed from the hips down, there was little the doctors or the family could do. He recovered from the fever, but it took months for him to learn how to stand or take a few steps on his own.

Sara and Eleanor Roosevelt joined forces to nurse Roosevelt during his recovery, but they disagreed about what he should do next. His mother hoped that he would retire from politics and settle with his family at Hyde Park, where he could live as a country gentleman. Eleanor, supported by Louis Howe, understood that Franklin would be miserable if he retired from politics. In September, they quietly moved him to Presbyterian Hospital in New York City to begin rehabilitation. They were afraid that if the public learned the extent of Franklin's disability, he would lose support in future elections. In the meantime, he began a long, painful process of building up his strength.

In October, he returned to the family home on 65th Street in New York City and began plotting his political future with Eleanor and Louis Howe. Their first task was to keep his name before the public. Roosevelt began writing letters to Democrats all over the nation, while Howe made political visits and Eleanor kept in touch with groups that had supported his campaigns.

Unable to walk, Franklin soon devised an armless chair with wheels that allowed him to move about the house. He played with his children by lying on the

The Conquest of Polio

Roosevelt devoted much of his inheritance to establishing a rehabilitation center at Warm Springs, Georgia. When he became president, he invited the public to contribute to his Warm Springs Foundation. After polio epidemics struck during the 1930s, President Roosevelt set up the National Foundation for Infantile Paralysis (another name for polio), to raise funds to treat patients and support medical research. Comedian Eddie Cantor asked people to send their dimes to the White House and coined the phase "March of Dimes." This became the foundation's official name. In the late 1950s, thanks to support from the March of Dimes, medical researchers developed a vaccine that could protect children from polio. Today nearly all children receive polio vaccine and need not fear being struck by the dread disease.

☆ ★ ☆

floor and wrestling with them. Knowing that he could not go up or down stairs on his own, his one great fear was fire. To overcome this, he taught himself to crawl across the floor from his bed to a window.

In January 1922, plaster casts were applied to his legs to keep unused muscles from tightening. Later, he was fitted for steel braces, weighing 14 pounds (6.35 kilograms), that stretched from his hips to his feet and helped support his upper body. While other Americans were learning new dances like the Charleston, Roosevelt was painfully learning to walk short distances with help. He arranged for a car at Hyde Park to be modified with hand controls. When he visited there, he was delighted to be able to get around the village on his own. Local residents were less pleased, since Roosevelt drove recklessly, often frightening pedestrians (and his passengers) with daredevil stops and starts.

In 1924, Roosevelt found that swimming at Warm Springs, Georgia, improved his condition. The warmth helped relax his muscles, and the water helped bear his weight. "I walk around in water four feet [1.2 meters] deep without braces and crutches," he wrote to his family. He built a cottage near the springs and would visit often for the rest of his life. He also established the Warm Springs Foundation, which helped pay the expenses of other polio sufferers who might be helped by the warm waters.

As Roosevelt recovered from polio, he found that warm water soothed his paralyzed legs and allowed him to exercise.

The Politician Returns

Roosevelt returned to the national spotlight at the 1924 Democratic convention in New York City. He gave an important nominating speech for Governor Al Smith of New York, describing the popular Irish-American governor as "the happy warrior of the political battlefield," and setting off a demonstration for Smith that lasted more than an hour. The convention deadlocked between the party's Northern liberals and its Southern conservatives. The convention lasted for 16 days as the delegates ran through 103 ballots before nominating John W. Davis, a compromise candidate. While the Democrats remained divided, the Republicans united behind President Calvin Coolidge, and he easily won the election.

In 1928 Al Smith won the Democratic nomination for president just as he was completing his fourth term as governor of New York. He urged Franklin Roosevelt to run for governor that fall. At first Roosevelt was reluctant, but he realized he might not have such an opportunity again, and he finally agreed. His first task was to convince voters in New York that he was healthy and up to the job. He waged an energetic campaign, appearing in scores of cities and towns and speaking to thousands. Roosevelt won by a slim margin of 25,000 votes. In the presidential election, Al Smith was soundly defeated for president by Republican Herbert Hoover.

The Governor and the Great Depression ———

Governor Roosevelt took office on January 1, 1929. That fall, the confidence of investors in the stock market faltered, and the value of stocks in major companies crashed. Like most Americans, Roosevelt had no idea that the country was headed for the disastrous economic downturn later known as the Great Depression.

After some improvement in the economy in early 1930, the economy went into a steep decline that fall. The stock market crashed again, and major companies began to fail, laying off their workers and going out of business. By early 1931, thousands of Americans were unemployed. Breadlines and soup kitchens opened to feed those who could not pay for food. Those who lost their homes moved to shantytowns on vacant lots, building shacks from castoff wood and sheet metal. They called the settlements "Hoovervilles," reflecting their anger with President Hoover for refusing to support direct government help for the unemployed and homeless. He promised that things would get better, but they did not.

Roosevelt was elected to a second term in 1930 by a margin of more than 750,000 votes. He pledged to take stronger action against the Depression. He expanded government work projects such as road building, offering jobs to some of the unemployed. He sent Eleanor out on field trips to gather information on conditions in various parts of the state. In August 1931, he established the

By 1932 the Depression was causing widespread suffering. These unemployed men in New York City are waiting in line for food provided by a private charity.

Temporary Emergency Relief Administration, which provided direct aid to families and individuals in serious need. It was directed by Harry Hopkins, a former social worker, who became an influential adviser to Roosevelt. By 1932, as the Depression deepened, the relief administration was paying an average of $23 a month (about $250 in present-day value) to about one New York family in ten. Nationwide, about 13 million people were out of work.

Presidential Campaign

Roosevelt's actions in New York attracted attention across the country. Soon after his re-election in 1930, he and his advisers began gathering support for a presidential run in 1932. A leading adviser was James Farley, who had directed Roosevelt's two campaigns for governor. Louis Howe continued to handle publicity. In addition, Roosevelt recruited a "Brain Trust" of university professors to recommend actions to cure the ailing economy.

Roosevelt's supporters came to the Democratic convention in 1932 with a *majority* (more than half) of delegate votes, but to gain the nomination they needed the support of two-thirds of the delegates. Two other candidates held most of the remaining votes—Al Smith, Roosevelt's old colleague from New York, and conservative congressman John Nance Garner of Texas. After the third ballot,

Roosevelt's campaign team persuaded Garner to give his delegate support to Roosevelt, and Roosevelt won the nomination on the fourth ballot. In return, Garner received the nomination for vice president.

Roosevelt appeared in person at the convention to make his acceptance speech. "I pledge you, I pledge myself, to a new deal for the American people," he told the delegates. A "new deal" became the theme of his campaign.

Once again, Roosevelt campaigned energetically. He condemned the empty words and inaction of President Hoover, offering instead a program to relieve the suffering of the needy, reform government operations, and help reconstruct the economy. Many Americans, including President Hoover, believed that the government should avoid interfering with business and that it should leave relief of the poor to private charities. Roosevelt intended to break with these traditions. It was clear to him that the government must take on new roles.

The broad outlines of Roosevelt's campaign promises were clear, but the details were not. He told an old friend, "Let's concentrate upon one thing—save the people and the nation, and if we have to change our minds twice every day to accomplish that end, we should do it."

On election day in November 1932, Roosevelt won 22.8 million votes to President Hoover's 15.8 million. He won in 42 of the 48 states. In the *electoral*

Roosevelt campaigns for president in 1932 with his vice-presidential running mate, Texan John Nance Garner.

college, the group of electors from each state that casts the official vote for president, Roosevelt received 472 electoral votes to Hoover's 59. His resounding victory also helped elect dozens of new Democratic members to Congress. Now a handicapped president would seek to help a country paralyzed by the most severe Depression in its history.

Chapter 4

Crisis

Between Roosevelt's election in November 1932 and his inauguration on March 4, 1933, economic conditions became even worse. The Great Depression now affected much of the world, causing new shocks at home. In the first months of 1933, more than 4,000 U.S. banks, with deposits of $3.6 billion, had failed. Panicky depositors had tried to withdraw all their money, but the banks ran out of cash, closed their doors, and went out of business. Franklin Roosevelt was sworn in as president at a moment of national crisis.

In his inaugural address, Roosevelt sounded a note of optimism and confidence. "This great nation will endure as it has endured, will revive, and will prosper," he said. "So, first of all, let me assert my firm belief that the only thing we have to fear is fear itself—nameless, unreasoning, unjustified terror which paralyzes needed

On inauguration day, March 4, 1933, Roosevelt rides to the ceremonies with outgoing president Herbert Hoover.

efforts to convert retreat into advance." He also announced his first action, calling Congress into a special session to begin the following week.

Even before Congress met, Roosevelt declared a "bank holiday," ordering all banks in the country to close for four days. The closings would give federal bank examiners a chance to begin studying banks' records to see which ones could reopen, which needed to be reorganized, and which were too hopelessly in debt to stay in business. He presented the Emergency Banking Act to Congress, with regulations that imposed many new restrictions on the banking system. Congress passed the act in a single day, extending the bank holiday for another

Fireside Chats

Roosevelt developed a new informal style in his radio addresses, saying that he thought of his audience as "a few people around his fireside." His language was natural and simple, and he took time to explain. On March 12, 1933, he explained the banking system: "When you deposit money in a bank, the bank does not put the money into a safe-deposit vault. It invests your money." He went on to explain the banks' problems and what he planned to do to help solve them.

Roosevelt addresses the nation by radio in one of his fireside chats.

In his twelve years as president, Roosevelt delivered nearly 30 fireside chats to explain New Deal programs, to win public support for his policies, and sometimes to calm fearful Americans. Roosevelt was the first president to use radio as an important way to stay in touch with the country's citizens.

☆ ★ ☆

business week. In the meantime, Roosevelt himself addressed the nation by radio to explain the situation. It was the first of many "fireside chats" he would deliver in the years to come.

The Emergency Bank Act succeeded in restoring confidence. By the end of March, three-fourths of banks reopened. The bank act also created an insurance program to protect money in personal bank accounts. If a bank failed, the insurance fund would repay depositors up to $2,500 (about $35,000 in present-day value).

The Hundred Days

Congress remained in session from March 9 to June 16. During this time it passed more than a dozen important bills extending the activity and powers of the government and addressing the Great Depression. During this "Hundred Days," the Roosevelt administration passed more far-reaching legislation than some administrations had passed in eight years.

Congress helped the jobless. Through the Civilian Conservation Corps, the government offered employment to jobless young adults. They planted forests, built roads, and worked on flood control. Federal grants helped employ construction workers building such huge public works as the Grand Coulee Dam

The Civilian Conservation Corps put many thousands of the unemployed to work on government projects. This crew is working at Rock Camp in California.

Repeal

In 1919, the 18th Amendment to the Constitution took effect, making it illegal to make, sell, or drink alcoholic beverages in the United States. *Prohibition*, as it was called, was considered an important step toward reducing crime and protecting families by ending alcohol abuse. By 1932, Prohibition was widely considered a failure, even by many who once supported it. Alcoholic beverages were still available, and now they were sold by gangsters, who became rich and powerful from their illegal trade. Gang wars were causing serious crimes to increase, and thousands of drinkers were dying from liquor that contained poisonous chemicals. A movement grew to *repeal*, or cancel, Prohibition. In February 1933, before Roosevelt took office, Congress passed a *Repeal* amendment. Repeal was so popular that 36 of 48 states ratified (approved) the amendment in less than ten months. On December 5, 1933, Roosevelt proclaimed the end of Prohibition.

☆ ☆ ☆

in Washington State and the Triborough Bridge in New York City. Another huge federal program was the Tennessee Valley Authority (TVA), which built a series of dams on the Tennessee River to provide inexpensive electricity and flood control to residents of six states. The TVA continues to manage the vast system.

Reimagining Government

In 1935, Roosevelt returned to a theme he had first sounded as New York governor. He proposed a government-administered insurance program called Social

Security. The government would take a special tax out of the wages of workers for this program. In return, workers would receive monthly benefits if they became disabled or when they retired. If a worker died before retirement, his or her family would receive benefits. The new program met strong resistance, but New Deal supporters overcame objections and passed the act. The Social Security system continues to operate today.

The administration offered strong support to workingmen and women, backing the rights of workers to organize unions and negotiate with their employers over working conditions and wages. The National Labor Relations Act, passed in 1935, provided protections for these activities and created the National Labor Relations Board to investigate labor disputes and supervise union elections. Roosevelt had also appointed Frances Perkins as secretary of labor. She was the first woman to head a federal department and to sit in the president's *cabinet*, or group of official advisers.

One of the most difficult problems for the New Deal was helping farmers, many of whom were losing their farms because of low crop prices. In 1933 Congress passed the Agricultural Adjustment Act (AAA), which paid farmers *not* to raise some crops until prices for them increased. The plan was controversial, and its opponents challenged the act in court. In 1936, the U.S. Supreme Court ruled that the AAA violated the Constitution and ordered that it be ended.

Above, a huge dust storm in Stratford, Texas, in 1935. Such storms turned the Great Plains into a "Dust Bowl," forcing thousands to leave the region to find work and food. Inset, a Dust Bowl family heading west along a rutted gravel road.

Roosevelt's New Dealers rushed to find new ways to help failing farmers that the court would consider constitutional.

In 1935, President Roosevelt signed an executive order establishing the Works Progress Administration (WPA), which soon became the largest federal employment program. Most of the WPA's projects involved manual labor, including new highway construction, reforestation, and slum clearance. Smaller WPA programs were organized especially for unemployed writers, artists, and musicians. The Federal Writers' Project prepared detailed guides to every state in the Union. Visual artists helped decorate hundreds of public buildings in every state. In its eight years of existence, the WPA spent more than $11 billion and employed 8.5 million different people at one time or another.

A Powerful President

Franklin Roosevelt seemed to relish his job. Even during a crisis, he seemed to look forward to each new day and each new challenge. In the White House, he managed the government's affairs in a relaxed and sometimes confusing manner. Often he assigned similar tasks to two or more assistants, asking them each to report their results. The assistants were often unhappy to learn that someone else was duplicating their work, but Roosevelt learned from each report, often combining the best from each. He used his charm to smooth his assistants' ruffled feathers.

Eleanor Roosevelt became her husband's eyes and ears, traveling to observe government programs across the country. Here she visits a government work program in Iowa.

These assignments were part of Roosevelt's strategy to keep information and opinions flowing to him. One of his most reliable "reporters" was Eleanor. She traveled widely, visiting WPA sites, and talking with local politicians and directors of special-interest groups. Once she even went down a mine shaft to see what conditions were like for coal miners. On a sad note, Roosevelt lost his closest adviser and assistant in 1936. Louis Howe, who had always been sickly, became critically ill and died. As president, Roosevelt now had his pick of advisers, but he could never quite replace Howe, who had worked with him for 25 years.

A Second Term

In 1936 Roosevelt ran for a second term against Republican Alfred Landon, the governor of Kansas. Landon condemned the New Deal as un-American. Roosevelt did not respond. At the Democratic convention that summer, he challenged Democrats to complete and strengthen the New Deal and to continue to defend it against its enemies. On election day, Roosevelt won 61 percent of the vote and every state except Maine and Vermont.

Roosevelt was inaugurated to his second term on January 20, 1937. He was the first president to be sworn in on a new date under the 20th Amendment to the Constitution, which moved the inauguration date back from early March to late January. In his second inaugural address, Roosevelt challenged the nation to help complete the work of his first term. Despite the progress made, he said, "I see one-third of a nation ill-housed, ill-clad, ill-nourished."

Weeks after his inauguration, Roosevelt unveiled a new and surprising plan to reorganize the nation's courts. Stung by court decisions against New Deal programs, he believed it was time to make the courts more responsive. His special target was the U.S. Supreme Court, which he once characterized as "nine old men." Roosevelt asked Congress to require judges to retire at age 70. If a judge refused to retire, the president wanted the right to appoint an additional judge (whose vote could offset the vote of the old judge).

The country's response to the plan was a resounding "No!" Roosevelt's enemies called it "court-packing," and suggested that the president was planning to set up a dictatorship, in which he controlled both Congress and the courts. Many loyal Democrats also backed away from the plan, considering it too radical. The Senate refused to pass the president's proposal, and he dropped it.

The court revision plan was a serious defeat and caused many citizens to question their support for the president. In the next few years, however, a number of judges died or retired. Roosevelt appointed judges more likely to consider his programs legally acceptable, and fewer of his programs were challenged by courts.

Even as the court battle was going on, the economy faltered once again, and many of the earlier gains of the New Deal were wiped out. New Dealers continued to pursue their programs. For the first time, the government set a minimum wage for workers and limited the number of hours in a week a worker could be required to work. Other acts took steps to outlaw child labor and dangerous working conditions.

Meanwhile the president continued to play his role as head of state, welcoming distinguished visitors from around the world. In 1938, King George VI and Queen Elizabeth of Great Britain made a state visit to Washington. Afterward they attended a picnic at Hyde Park. That summer, the Roosevelts also

Shirley Temple

Shirley Temple (born 1928) was a Hollywood star at the age of six. With her hair in ringlets, her bright smile, and dimples, she often played an abandoned child who never gave in to despair. In films like *Baby Take a Bow* and *Curly Top*, she sang and danced her way to a happy ending while popularizing such songs as "The Good Ship Lollipop." Her movies helped Americans take their minds off their troubles. President Roosevelt liked her "infectious optimism" and claimed that "as long as our country has Shirley Temple, we will be all right."

Young Shirley Temple, a movie sensation in the 1930s, visits with Eleanor Roosevelt.

Shirley Temple retired from films when she reached 20, married, and raised a family. She later served under presidents Nixon, Ford, and Bush as a delegate to the United Nations and as ambassador to Ghana and Czechoslovakia.

☆ ☆ ☆

entertained Hollywood royalty, the most famous child actor of the day, 10-year-old Shirley Temple.

Isolation and Neutrality ——————————————

By 1937, President Roosevelt was concentrating more and more on foreign affairs.

Dictator Adolf Hitler had taken over the government of Germany. Hitler taught

that the German race was superior to others. He believed that Germany had been

unfairly forced to give up territory after World War I, and he was building a huge

army to help get it back. He blamed Germany's problems on other "inferior races,"

especially Jews. He limited the rights of Jews and others in Germany to practice

certain professions, to attend schools, and to live where they chose. Many Jews left

the country to escape his persecution, but many thousands remained.

Hitler had formed an alliance with Italy, ruled by dictator Benito

Mussolini, in 1936. Together, they were known as the Axis powers. Mussolini

was eager to gain new territories for his country. In 1936 his armies occupied

Ethiopia in northeastern Africa. Meanwhile, Japan had built a powerful army and

navy and was threatening its neighbors in Asia. It had already captured the

Chinese province of Manchuria in 1931. Beginning in 1937, it began a campaign

to capture major Chinese cities.

Roosevelt was deeply concerned about these developments. Many Ameri-

cans were *isolationists*, however. They believed that the United States should not

take sides or get involved in foreign quarrels. In October 1937, Roosevelt chal-

lenged these isolationists. In a speech in Chicago, he warned starkly, "The

German Chancellor Adolf Hitler, whose armies were threatening surrounding countries, addresses a huge rally in Berlin in 1938.

epidemic of world lawlessness is spreading." He urged Americans to join with other peace-loving peoples to "quarantine" the offending nations before their lawlessness spread further. Public reaction to the speech was cool. Isolationists warned that Roosevelt's approach would involve the country in another war. Other people just seemed unconcerned. Roosevelt was discouraged. He said to his aides, "It's a terrible thing to look over your shoulder when you are trying to lead—and find no one there."

World War

In early 1938, Germany took over neighboring Austria. Later that year, frightened European nations agreed that Germany could occupy part of Czechoslovakia. In November, mobs organized by Hitler's government destroyed the shops and businesses of Jews throughout Germany.

Early in 1939, Germany took over the government of all Czechoslovakia and began preparations to invade Poland. The British and French, who had hoped Hitler would be satisfied with his earlier conquests, realized that he hoped to conquer all of Europe. On September 1, German armies marched into Poland. Days later, Britain and France declared war. The United States issued a statement of neutrality.

In 1939 Hitler observes as the German army marches across Poland. The German invasion on September 1 marked the beginning of World War II.

Roosevelt considered Germany and Japan serious threats to the United States and was worried about the survival of the Allied nations, but pressure was still strong to stay out of the war. The president struggled to find a way to assist Britain and France, which were now under direct attack by Germany. By the end of June 1940, France was occupied by German armies, and British forces had been driven out of Europe. In July, Hitler began a bombing and terror campaign against Britain.

At last, the United States began to mobilize for war. Roosevelt gained approval from Congress to sell war materials to allies abroad, provided buyers paid cash and carried the goods away in their own ships. In September 1940, Congress also passed a military conscription law, enabling the government to draft men into military service.

Roosevelt soon formed a personal friendship with Prime Minister Winston Churchill of Great Britain. In September 1940, Roosevelt arranged to "lend" 50 old U.S. destroyers to Britain in exchange for long-term leases to old British military bases. Britain needed the destroyers to withstand German submarine attacks on its shipping. Roosevelt did not need the leases, but the trade allowed him to complete the deal without gaining congressional approval, which might have taken months. Roosevelt described America's role in a fireside chat late that year. "We must become the arsenal of democracy," he said.

As huge new government expenditures were made for production of war supplies, more and more Americans found jobs. By the end of 1940, unemployment had nearly disappeared. The government had to borrow huge amounts to pay for the new manufacturing, but those bills would not come due until after the war was over.

A Third Term

In this ominous year, Democrats and Republicans were preparing for a presidential election. President Roosevelt had a serious problem. He was completing his second term in the White House, and no other president had ever been elected to a third term. Deeply involved in the critical world situation, Roosevelt wanted to run for another term, but he knew that if he seemed eager for it, critics would accuse him again of wanting to be a dictator. He had to wait for his party to "draft" him.

Roosevelt sent mixed messages to his supporters. On the one hand, he arranged to send presidential papers and records to Hyde Park, suggesting that he planned to retire. On the other hand, he quietly encouraged party leaders to push for his nomination at the Democratic convention. When his name was placed in nomination, it set off a huge demonstration. He was nominated on the first ballot.

The Republicans nominated Wendell Willkie. Even though many Republicans were isolationists, Willkie was a strong supporter of U.S. aid to Allied nations.

Willkie did criticize Roosevelt's New Deal programs, however, and other Republicans campaigned against Roosevelt—or any other president—being elected for a third term. Roosevelt was easily re-elected. A majority of voters trusted him to face a world crisis at least as threatening as the Great Depression had been. He received 27 million popular votes to Willkie's 22 million and 449 electoral votes to Willkie's 82.

Roosevelt's run for a third term as president in 1940 caused heated debate. His opponents claimed he was becoming a king (above). His supporters claimed his election was necessary as war threatened the nation (right).

Chapter 5

Goals for the Nation and Its Allies ——

Even before he was inaugurated, Roosevelt was lobbying Congress to pass an act that would allow the United States to lend or lease equipment to Britain and other allies. Britain was running out of money to pay for war equipment but still needed it desperately. At a press conference in December 1940, the president explained with a simple story:

> Suppose my neighbor's home catches on fire and I have a length of garden hose four or five hundred feet away. If he can take my garden hose and connect it to his hydrant, I may be able to help put out his fire. . . . Now I don't say to him before that operation, "Neighbor, my garden hose cost me $15, you have to pay me $15 for it." . . . I don't want $15. I want my garden hose back after the fire is over.

Even though it was clear that many of the supplies lent to the Allies would never be returned, the story emphasized the seriousness of the occasion. Britain (our neighbor) was in grave danger. On March 11, 1941, Congress passed the Lend-Lease Act, allowing the sale, exchange, or lease of arms and equipment. Public opinion was shifting in favor of joining the war.

In his State of the Union address to Congress in January 1941, Roosevelt went further than ever in urging Americans to take sides in the war. He outlined the values he believed were at stake, not only in the United States but worldwide. Near the end of his solemn address, he listed "four essential human freedoms." They were freedom of speech, freedom to worship, freedom from want, and freedom from fear. He presented them as freedoms worth fighting for and worth bringing to the rest of the world.

In August, Roosevelt took what appeared to be an innocent cruise in the North Atlantic, not far from his summer home at Campobello. In reality, he met another ship off the coast of Nova Scotia and held a secret conference with Prime Minister Churchill. The two leaders worked out a document inspired by the "four freedoms" which they called the Atlantic Charter. It described what the Allies were fighting for and the world they envisioned at the end of the war. Among the aims were freedom of the seas, the right of peoples to freely choose their government, greater international trade, improved working conditions and retirement benefits for labor, and a lasting peace without territorial conquests. The charter also called for an international organization of nations to help prevent future wars and encourage peace.

Pearl Harbor

In September, Sara Roosevelt died, a few weeks before her 87th birthday. Roosevelt's mother had been a central person in his life. He canceled his appointments and secluded himself at Hyde Park to mourn her death. After a few days, however, he returned to his presidential duties, knowing that the world would not stop for a grieving president.

In July, the powerful German war machine invaded the Soviet Union and soon forced the Soviets to retreat hundreds of miles. At the same time, they carried out a brutal bombing campaign against Britain. There were also ominous signs of war in the Pacific. Japan, which already controlled much of China, was moving into present-day Vietnam and Thailand, and was planning to attack the Philippines, then a U.S. possession. Japan was frustrated that the United States refused to sell it raw materials needed for its war efforts. In December, Japanese diplomats were in Washington discussing disagreements between the two countries.

On Sunday afternoon, December 7, 1941, President Roosevelt was in his study awaiting an official response from the Japanese visitors. At 1:40, he received a phone call from Secretary of the Navy Frank Knox, reporting that the U.S. naval base in Pearl Harbor, Hawaii, was under attack by Japanese bombers. Through the afternoon, reports continued to come in. The surprise attack, mounted from aircraft carriers, occurred early Sunday morning Hawaii time, catching the U.S. fleet at anchor in the bay and many of the sailors asleep. Eighteen warships were sunk or badly damaged, and 188 airplanes were destroyed, most of them on the ground. Worst of all, more than 2,400 U.S. servicemen were killed.

About five o'clock, Roosevelt summoned secretary Grace Tully to his study. He wanted to dictate a message, which he would read in person to Congress. The next day, December 8, the president appeared before a joint session and read his brief statement. It began:

> Yesterday, December 7, 1941—a date which will live in infamy—the
>
> United States of America was suddenly and deliberately attacked by
>
> naval and air forces of the Empire of Japan.

The statement went on to request a declaration of war on Japan. Congress passed the war declaration later that day. Three days later, Germany and Italy declared war on the United States. The country had entered the most threatening foreign war in its history.

The USS *Arizona* burns at its moorings in Hawaii's Pearl Harbor after the surprise attack by Japanese bombers on December 7, 1941. The following day, the United States declared war on Japan.

Taking Up Arms

On the day of the attack, the United States already had about 1.9 million men in the military service, including all four of Franklin Roosevelt's sons. Within weeks there would be hundreds of thousands more. It would take time, however, to train and equip this vast force and send it to distant theaters of war. In the meantime, U.S. defense industries continued to provide huge quantities of war supplies to Britain, the Soviet Union, and other Allied troops.

War brought major changes to American society. For the first time, women were allowed to volunteer for noncombat positions in the military service, and more than 200,000 joined by war's end. Women were also encouraged to take jobs in defense industries, taking the place of men who had joined the armed forces. Recruiters invented "Rosie the Riveter," a character who symbolized the working women who would contribute to the war effort.

Even before Pearl Harbor, President Roosevelt set up the Fair Employment Practices Commission to outlaw discrimination based on race or color in hiring for defense industries. Hundreds of thousands of African Americans were hired. More than 900,000 also served in the armed forces. Both white and black officer candidates attended the same training schools, but most fighting units were still segregated—they were white-only or black-only. Some groups made

As millions of men were sent overseas to fight, women took an important new role at home. This poster featuring "Rosie the Riveter" urges women to take jobs in defense industries.

special contributions. Members of several Native American tribes used their native languages as code to send messages in sensitive areas.

After Pearl Harbor, many people feared that Japanese Americans might not be loyal and might pass military information to their ancestral country. U.S. authorities began rounding up Japanese Americans, and President Roosevelt signed an executive order setting up residential camps for them in remote areas far from the Pacific shore. About 120,000 Japanese-born citizens and their children were kept under guard in these camps for the remainder of the war. They were fed and cared for, but they were held without charges simply because they were of Japanese heritage. After the war, many returned to their former homes to find their houses and businesses sold. A commission established in the 1980s concluded that the internment of Japanese Americans was an injustice and recommended that each surviving person be paid $20,000 as a token of apology. Even as their families were interned in special camps, some Japanese Americans served with distinction and bravery in the U.S. armed forces.

Another front in the war was science and research. In 1939, world-famous physicist Albert Einstein sent a letter to President Roosevelt warning that German researchers might be studying *nuclear fission*, the splitting of atoms, as a source of energy for a huge bomb. Roosevelt ordered increased research on atomic weapons. An international team of scientists proved that such a weapon was possible, and beginning in 1942, the U.S. government mounted a huge secret effort to build and test an atomic bomb. Other scientific labs invented or helped develop radar and sonar, which could be used to track enemy vessels in the sky or sea.

Commander in Chief ————————————

Roosevelt told the press in 1942 that he was no longer "Dr. New Deal." Now he was "Dr. Win-the-War." As commander in chief, he faced a daunting task. German armies had conquered most of Europe and the western Soviet Union. The Japanese had overrun key islands and cities in the Pacific. The United States was supplying huge amounts of war materiel to its allies in Europe, and now it was faced with a long and difficult battle across endless tracts of sea against Japan. The president set his first priority as supplying Britain to keep up its battle against Germany, postponing any major offensives in the Pacific.

Even without huge resources, the war against Japan got off to a good start. U.S. forces won important naval battles in the Coral Sea in May and near the Midway Islands in June. In August 1942, U.S. troops attacked the Japanese stronghold at Guadalcanal, one of the Solomon Islands. A bitter fight against determined Japanese defenders took more than six months. Finally, in February 1943, U.S. troops secured the island. From then on, U.S. hopped from island to island. They bypassed many Japanese strongholds, then cut the supply lines, leaving the strongholds to run out of ammunition and food.

Meanwhile, Roosevelt accepted Churchill's proposal to send U.S. troops to North Africa to reinforce the British troops there in Operation Torch. British forces moving west from Egypt had been fighting a difficult campaign against German and Italian troops. The new British and American troops landed in Morocco in November 1942 and pushed eastward, hoping to trap the Axis army between two Allied armies. American forces were inexperienced, but they contributed to defeating the Axis in North Africa in May 1943.

In January 1943, Roosevelt and Churchill met in Casablanca in Allied-occupied Morocco. They discussed strategy for the remainder of the war and agreed that the Allies would require the Axis powers to surrender unconditionally before fighting would end. There would be no negotiated settlement. The two leaders also agreed that the next Allied campaign would be the invasion of Sicily, a first step in gaining possession of all Italy. Soviet leader Joseph Stalin, who did not come to Casablanca, was bitterly disappointed by their decision. He had hoped for a much larger invasion of German-occupied France, which would reduce the pressure on his armies. Roosevelt and Churchill put off an invasion of France until 1944.

The First Presidential Airplane

President Roosevelt loved sea travel, but during wartime, it was too dangerous and too slow. Eleanor Roosevelt, who enjoyed traveling by air, encouraged him to take his first flight to the Allied conference in Casablanca. Roosevelt flew in a Boeing 314 Clipper to the conference, becoming the first president to fly overseas while in office. When he returned home, he arranged for the construction of a special plane to carry him to later conferences. This C-54 Skymaster was nicknamed the *Sacred Cow*.

☆ ☆ ☆

The Allied invasion of Sicily, Operation Husky, began on July 9, 1943. Less than six weeks later, in mid-August, the Allies had secured the island. In September they attacked the Italian mainland. Fighting there would be hard and costly, and they would not occupy Rome, the Italian capital, until the summer of 1944.

In November 1943, Roosevelt traveled once again to meet with the other Allied leaders in Tehran, the capital of Iran. Roosevelt and Churchill agreed to schedule an invasion of France for the late spring of 1944. Stalin agreed to begin a new offensive on the eastern front at about the same time. The Allied forces would soon be closing in on Germany itself.

Operation Overlord, the invasion of the coast of Normandy in western France, finally began on June 6, 1944. The largest invasion by sea in history, it

President Roosevelt (center) met with other powerful Allied leaders at Tehran, Iran, in 1943. Josef Stalin (left) was the leader of the Soviet Union, and Winston Churchill (right) was prime minister of Great Britain.

involved more than 175,000 Allied troops, 4,000 landing craft, 600 warships, and nearly 10,000 planes. American and British forces successfully crossed the stormy English Channel. Then, under constant German bombardment, they gained a foothold on the mainland of Western Europe. In the following weeks, they would drive the Germans across France, liberating Paris on August 25. Meanwhile, Soviet armies were driving the Germans out of Soviet territories. Slowly, the Allies were winning the war.

U.S. troops wade through the surf to the beach at Normandy in northern France on June 6, 1944. Allied troops soon drove German forces out of France.

FDR's Health

Early in 1944, Roosevelt's health began to decline. He often felt exhausted and had occasional chest pains. In a checkup in March 1944, doctors found that he had serious heart disease. They prescribed medication for his chest pain and advised him to take a long vacation. Even a month in Warm Springs did not bring complete recovery. He adopted a less demanding work schedule and a new diet, but he still was often tired and had trouble concentrating. Eleanor later wrote, "I think we all knew that Franklin was far from well, but none of us ever said anything about it—I suppose because we felt that if he believed it was his duty to continue in office, there was nothing for us to do but make it as easy as possible for him."

Election of 1944

In late 1943, Roosevelt turned his attention to preparing for peace. His advisers told him that when millions of veterans returned from the war and defense industries ended their round-the-clock production, there would be widespread unemployment and frustration. To offer some repayment to veterans for their courageous service and to avoid possible unemployment at war's end, the administration prepared a far-reaching veterans' benefit package. It received enthusiastic support from veterans' groups at home and was passed by Congress in mid-June, weeks after the successful Allied invasion of France. The bill, which

Eleanor Roosevelt (1884–1962) was quite different from most earlier first ladies. She went far beyond serving as White House hostess to become a powerful advocate for African American civil rights, public assistance for the unemployed, and other controversial causes. She regularly argued these causes directly with the president. She was the first president's wife to work independently, writing newspaper and magazine columns and hosting a radio program. In 1941 she briefly held a government post as well.

Eleanor Roosevelt visits with military leaders in the South Pacific during the war. The plane in the background is named "Our Eleanor."

In many of her activities she served as Franklin Roosevelt's eyes and ears. She traveled coast to coast in the 1930s, visiting New Deal programs, meeting with concerned citizens, and consulting with political leaders. During World War II, she traveled overseas to review the military situation and to visit U.S. troops. She and her husband generally agreed on government policies and programs, but she never hesitated to speak out when she disagreed with him.

After Franklin's death, Eleanor Roosevelt continued her activities. She became a delegate to the United Nations and helped to write its Universal Declaration of Human Rights. She wrote a regular newspaper column for many years and became an important elder statesman in the Democratic party.

She was perhaps the most controversial first lady up to her time. She had many supporters who cheered her independence and her activism. At the same time, many Americans disliked her, accusing her of meddling in public affairs and paying too little attention to her duties as White House hostess. She did not suit their image of a perfect first lady.

came to be known as the GI Bill, provided generous benefits to returning veterans for study (in colleges or job-training programs); guaranteed loans to help buy a home, a business, or a farm; and extended unemployment benefits for any who could not find a job. Roosevelt signed the bill on June 22, 1944.

The following month, Democrats met in convention to nominate a candidate for president. Roosevelt was already the first president to be serving his third term. Could he possibly run for a fourth term? Roosevelt had let party leaders know he wanted to run one last time and see the country through the war. They nominated him on the first ballot. The only drama involved the party's choice for vice president. Many leaders thought Henry Wallace, the current vice president, was too liberal, and they proposed "dumping" him for a more conservative candidate. Finally, to avoid a deadlock between New Dealers and conservatives, both sides agreed on Harry S. Truman, a senator from Missouri.

The Republicans nominated New York governor Thomas E. Dewey for president. He campaigned across the country, making Roosevelt's health a major issue. Roosevelt relied mainly on the radio to reach the public. He used humor to deflect criticisms by Republicans. He even reported that his beloved dog Fala was furious over Republican attacks. On election day, Roosevelt received 25.6 million popular votes and 432 electoral votes to Dewey's 22 million popular votes and 99

On the day of Roosevelt's inauguration to a fourth term in January 1945, he poses with Eleanor and their 13 grandchildren.

electoral votes. For the fourth time in his life, he listened to the election returns from Hyde Park and gave a victory speech to a crowd of neighbors and friends.

After a rest at Warm Springs, he returned to Washington, where he worked until a Christmas break at Hyde Park with his family. As usual, he read Dickens's *A Christmas Carol* to his 13 grandchildren. Three weeks later, all of them also attended his fourth inauguration in Washington. Because of security concerns, the president took the oath of office in a quiet ceremony at the White House, not during the usual outdoor celebration at the Capitol.

Yalta

Two days after the inauguration, Roosevelt left on the new presidential plane, the *Sacred Cow*, for a conference with Allied leaders Stalin and Churchill at Yalta, a resort city in the southern Soviet Union. Roosevelt gained an agreement from Stalin to help the Americans finish the war against Japan once Germany surrendered. Stalin also agreed that the Soviet Union would join the United Nations, the new world organization to help keep the peace. Other negotiations were more difficult. Stalin's armies occupied all of Poland, and he would not agree to hold truly open elections there, preferring to install a Communist government closely allied to the Soviet Union.

When Roosevelt returned home, he reported in person to Congress. For the first time, he sat while delivering his address. Members of Congress noticed

The United Nations

The United Nations was established by the Allied powers in the closing days of World War II to promote international peace and cooperation, and it continues in operation today. Its headquarters is in New York City, and it operates specialized offices in many world cities. The two main bodies for discussion and debate are the Security Council and the General Assembly. The Security Council has five permanent member nations and ten members that serve for limited terms. The council considers pressing matters of war and peace. The General Assembly is made up of all member nations. It discusses matters of common interest, elects judges of the World Court, and chooses members of UN councils and committees. The highest official in the UN is the secretary general, who manages the Secretariat, the organization's administrative staff.

UN membership has grown from 51 nations in 1945 to nearly 200 today. It has not always been able to keep peace in the world, but it continues to offer nations a forum where disputes can be resolved without resorting to war.

☆ ★ ☆

how pale and fragile he looked. His report stressed the organization of the United Nations, which he hoped would help put an end to secret alliances and treaties. Meanwhile Russian troops pressed farther into Germany from the east, aiming at Berlin. Americans were approaching the German capital, from the south and west.

Churchill, Roosevelt, and Stalin at the Yalta Conference in February 1945. Already seriously ill, Roosevelt died only two months later.

Death of a President

Early in April, Roosevelt traveled once again to Warm Springs for a vacation. He wanted to build up his strength so that he could open the founding conference of the United Nations at the end of the month. On the afternoon of April 12, he sat by the fireplace signing letters and official papers. A painter was at work on a watercolor portrait of him. About 1:15, Roosevelt complained, "I have a terrific headache." Then his head slumped over onto the table. A doctor put the unconscious president to bed. Roosevelt had suffered a *cerebral hemorrhage*, an interruption of blood flow to the brain, and nothing could be done to save him. He was declared dead at 3:35. The first bulletin announcing his death was broadcast about 5:45, and within an hour, most Americans knew their president had died.

Early that evening, Vice President Harry Truman was sworn in as president at a ceremony in the White House. In the following days, Eleanor Roosevelt escorted her husband's body back to Washington by train. Crowds lined the streets as his casket was taken to the White House for a brief service. Then the family and officials left by train for Hyde Park, where the late president was buried in the Rose Garden of his family's estate. Telegrams and letters poured in from across the nation and the world, paying tribute to Franklin Roosevelt and mourning his death.

Vice President Harry S. Truman is sworn in as president on April 12, 1945, hours after President Roosevelt died.

Unfinished Business ————————

By the end of April, Soviet troops were capturing Berlin street by street. Adolf Hitler, in a bunker below street level, committed suicide to avoid capture. On May 7, Germany formally surrendered, ending the war in Europe.

Fighting in the Pacific continued into the summer. American military leaders were planning a costly and hazardous invasion of Japan. Then on July 16, American scientists set off the first atomic bomb in history at a test site in New Mexico. It proved that an atomic bomb could be a devastating weapon. Within days, President Truman ordered the military to prepare to use one or more of the bombs against Japan. He and his advisers believed that the new weapon could shorten the war and reduce the death and destruction that an invasion of Japan would certainly cost.

Two atomic bombs were dropped on Japanese cities—on Hiroshima on August 6, and another on Nagasaki on August 9. Five days later, on August 14, President Truman announced that Japan had surrendered. The formal surrender ceremony was held September 2, 1945, aboard the battleship *Missouri* in Tokyo Bay.

Chapter 6

A Crisis President

Franklin Roosevelt's policies were controversial during his lifetime and some remain controversial today. Yet nearly every survey of historians ranks Roosevelt one of the five most effective presidents in U.S. history.

Roosevelt served longer than any other president in history, gaining election to four terms and serving for 12 years and 39 days. More important, he served during two of the great crises in American history. During the first half of his presidency, the country passed through its most severe economic depression, when millions were out of work and many were homeless and hungry. He did not succeed in ending the depression quickly, but he brought government aid to the suffering and helped adapt government to new circumstances.

During the second half of his presidency, the United States faced a critical challenge overseas. Its friends were threatened by the powerful war machines of Germany and Japan. Roosevelt worked tirelessly to persuade Americans to help the Allied nations and to prepare themselves for the possibility of war. When the United States entered the war, he helped plan Allied strategy and directed U.S. war production at home. He died only months before the great war ended in victory for the United States and its allies.

Domestic Policies

Roosevelt made a lasting mark on the U.S. government. He established government programs that provide pension payments for retired Americans and benefits for the disabled, dependent children, and the unemployed. Many later political leaders have criticized Roosevelt's initiatives, but these programs continue to be widely popular more than 60 years after his death.

Roosevelt's New Deal also increased the role of government in regulating business. It set up the Securities and Exchange Commission to protect individual investors against stock frauds and the National Labor Relations Board to protect workers' rights to form unions and negotiate with their employers. It set up federal insurance to protect deposits in individual bank accounts.

Franklin D. Roosevelt.

Roosevelt also led by personal example. As the first president with a serious physical disability, he spent much of his personal fortune establishing a rehabilitation site in Warm Springs, Georgia, for victims of polio and other paralytic conditions. Later, he led fund-raising for the treatment and prevention of polio. Years after his death, the charity he helped establish contributed to the development of a vaccine that protects future generations from the dread disease.

Many have also criticized some of Roosevelt's domestic actions before and during World War II. Some say he did not act forcefully enough to admit Jewish refugees in the 1930s or to stop the killing of Jews by German authorities during the war. Roosevelt knew that the government of Germany was persecuting Jews both in Germany and in the countries it captured. After the United States entered the war, he also learned of the special death camps Germans built to exterminate Jews and others they considered undesirable. He believed the best way to end the persecution and killing was to defeat Germany as soon as possible. Only after the war (and after Roosevelt's death) did the world realize the magnitude of the atrocities. In an act of *genocide*, the Germans sought to destroy all Jews in Europe, killing more than 6 million people in a network of work camps and special death camps.

Roosevelt also received stern criticism for his agreement to intern Japanese Americans as security risks after the attack on Pearl Harbor. The U.S.

government made payments to all Japanese Americans held in camps during the war and officially apologized to them during the 1980s.

Foreign Policies ————————————————

For many years United States policy had been isolationist, refusing to enter international treaties or participate in international organizations. As World War II approached, Roosevelt persuaded the country to break out of its isolation and recognize that it was an important member of the world community. Since his presidency, the United States has remained an active participant in international affairs.

Once the United States entered the war, Roosevelt worked closely with other Allied leaders to defeat their enemies and to establish a more peaceful world when the war ended. He was a main architect and supporter of the United Nations, which was established in the months after his death. The world body has often had strong critics in the United States, but the country remains a loyal and active member.

In the years after Roosevelt's death, the Soviet Union became an enemy and major competitor of the United States. Some historians blame Roosevelt for the "loss" of Eastern European countries (Poland, Czechoslovakia, Hungary, and others) to Communism. They claim he was too lenient in negotiating with Joseph

Roosevelt and Disability

When the Roosevelt Memorial opened, many disabled Americans were disappointed. The only the statue of the president shows him with a flowing cape, concealing his legs and his wheelchair. During his presidency, Roosevelt and his assistants refused to allow photographs of him in the wheelchair.

Spokesmen for the disabled argued forcefully that one image of Roosevelt at his memorial should show his disability. In January 2001, a new statue of the president in his wheelchair was unveiled. Nearby is a quotation from Eleanor Roosevelt, who said, "Franklin's illness gave him strength and courage he had not had before."

☆ ☆ ☆

Stalin in wartime conferences. However, Roosevelt did not have much power over Stalin's actions at the time, because Soviet armies occupied Eastern Europe.

The FDR Memorial

Franklin Roosevelt remains a familiar figure in American life. His face appears on every dime, and his legacy as a president during depression and war is well known. In 1997, after years of planning, the Roosevelt Memorial was opened in Washington, D.C. It takes its place with the Lincoln and Jefferson Memorials and the Washington Monument.

D) SEEK TO ESTABLISH
GOVERNMENT BASED ON
ENTATION OF ALL HUMAN
HANDFUL OF INDIVIDUAL
ALL THIS A NEW ORDER.
EW AND IT IS NOT ORDER.

A statue of the president and his dog Fala at the Franklin Delano Roosevelt Memorial in Washington, D.C.

The memorial represents Roosevelt's contributions in four galleries, one for each of his presidential terms. They contain bronze statues of a Depression breadline, a family listening to a fireside chat, Roosevelt during wartime (with his dog Fala), and Eleanor Roosevelt. On the walls are some of Roosevelt's inspiring statements and a timeline of important dates in his life.

The Roosevelt Memorial helps remind future generations about the legacy of this remarkable American. Through words and sculpture, it shows that a paralyzed man got America back on its feet during the Great Depression and led it to victory in World War II. It is no wonder that some historians and biographers consider him the greatest of all U.S. presidents.

Fast Facts Franklin Delano Roosevelt

Birth:	January 30, 1882
Birthplace:	Hyde Park, New York
Parents:	James Roosevelt and Sara Delano Roosevelt
Half Brother:	James Roosevelt Roosevelt (1854–1927)
Education:	Harvard University, graduated 1904
	Columbia University Law School, 1904–1907
Occupations:	Lawyer, state legislator, bank officer, governor
Marriage:	To Eleanor Roosevelt, March 17, 1905
Children:	(*see* First Lady Fast Facts at right)
Political Party:	Democratic
Public Offices:	1911–1913 New York State Senate
	1913–1920 Assistant Secretary of the Navy
	1929–1933 Governor of New York State
	1933–1945 32nd President of the United States
His Vice Presidents:	1933–1941 John Nance Garner
	1941–1945 Henry A. Wallace
	1945 Harry S. Truman
Major Actions as President:	March–June 1933 Signs key New Deal acts during the "Hundred Days"
	August 1935 Signs Social Security Act
	June 1938 Signs Fair Labor Standards Act
	September 1939 Proclaims U.S. neutrality after World War II begins in Europe
	September 1940 Trades 50 overage destroyers to Britain for leases to military bases
	January 1941 Gives "Four Freedoms" speech
	December 1941 Asks for declaration of war against Japan after Pearl Harbor attack; United States enters World War II
	August 1942 Issues Atlantic Charter with Churchill
	November–December 1943 Meets with Churchill and Stalin in Tehran, Iran
	June 1944 Signs GI Bill of Rights
	February 1945 Meets with Stalin and Churchill at Yalta
Firsts:	First and only president to be elected to four terms of office
	First president to travel overseas in wartime
Death:	April 12, 1945
Age at Death:	63 years
Burial Place:	Family plot in the Roosevelt estate at Hyde Park, New York

Fast Facts Anna Eleanor Roosevelt

Birth:	October 11, 1884
Birthplace:	New York, New York
Parents:	Elliott Roosevelt and Anna Livingston Hall Roosevelt
Education:	Allenswood, a girls' school near London, England, 1899–1902
Marriage:	To Franklin Delano Roosevelt, March 17, 1905
Children:	Anna Eleanor (1906–1975)
	James (1907–1991)
	Franklin (March 1909–November 1909)
	Elliott (1910–1990)
	Franklin Junior (1914–1988)
	John Aspinwall (1916–1981)
Firsts:	First president's wife to fly in an airplane to a foreign nation
	First to hold her own White House press conferences
	First to testify before a Senate committee
	First to hold a government job (in the Office of Civilian Defense)
	First to address a national political convention
Death:	November 7, 1962
Age at Death:	78 years
Burial Place:	Family plot in the Roosevelt estate at Hyde Park, New York

Timeline

1882	1896	1900	1904	1905
Franklin Delano Roosevelt born in Hyde Park, NY, January 30	Attends the Groton School in Massachusetts; graduates 1900	Enrolls at Harvard College; graduates 1904	Enters Columbia University Law School	Marries Anna Eleanor Roosevelt, March 17

1920	1921	1924	1928	1930
Returns to New York, practices law, and becomes bank officer	Stricken with poliomyelitis, August; begins long rehabilitation to deal with paralysis	Nominates New York governor Al Smith for president at Democratic convention	Elected governor of New York; Al Smith loses presidential election to Republican Herbert Hoover	Great Depression begins; Roosevelt re-elected governor

1939	1940	1941	1944	1945
World War II begins in Europe, September; Roosevelt proclaims United States is neutral	Re-elected to third term to address growing threat of war	Japan attacks U.S. base at Pearl Harbor, Hawaii, United States enters World War II, December	Roosevelt elected to fourth term as Allied forces close in on Germany and Japan	Inaugurated, January 20; dies in Warm Springs, Georgia, April 12

1907	1910	1912	1913	1920
Begins practice of law	Elected to the New York State Senate	Supports Woodrow Wilson for president; re-elected to state senate	Appointed assistant secretary of the navy by President Wilson	Runs for vice president with presidential candidate James M. Cox; they are defeated by Republicans Warren Harding and Calvin Coolidge

1932	1933	1935	1936	1937
Receives Democratic nomination for president; defeats Republican Hoover in election	Inaugurated, March; calls special session of Congress to address depression emergency, March–June	Signs Social Security Act	Re-elected to second term in landslide over Republican Alf Landon	Proposes plan to reorganize federal courts; proposal is defeated

1945

Germany surrenders to Allies, May 7; Japan surrenders August 14; United Nations begins operation

Glossary

★ ★ ★ ★ ★

bosses: political leaders who controlled political organizations that held power by exchanging government contracts and favors for money and votes

cabinet: the directors of federal government departments who meet to advise the president

cerebral hemorrhage: bleeding in the brain, which may cause paralysis or death

electoral college: the group of electors from each state and the District of Columbia that officially elects the U.S. president and vice president; the electors vote based on the popular vote in their states, and a majority of electors is required to elect

genocide: an organized effort to kill a whole people or nation

isolationists: people who believed that the United States should not take sides or intervene in foreign quarrels or make treaties with foreign governments

majority: in a vote, at least one more than half of the votes; in a legislature, the political party with a majority of votes has the right to choose the presiding officer and organize committees

neutral: during a war or other dispute, refusing to support or show favor to either side

nuclear fission: the splitting of an atom of matter, which releases terrific energy; a chain reaction in which many atoms are split provides the energy for nuclear weapons

poliomyelitis: also known as polio; a viral disease that can paralyze arms or legs or lungs, preventing them from functioning; it was sometimes called infantile paralysis because it affected so many young infants or children

Prohibition: the popular name for the 18th Amendment to the Constitution (1919) and laws passed to implement it; the amendment prohibited the manufacture, sale, or use of alcoholic beverages in the United States; *see also* Repeal

Repeal: the popular name for the 21st Amendment to the Constitution (1933), which repealed, or canceled, Prohibition

Further Reading

Kudlinski, Kathleen. *Franklin Delano Roosevelt.* New York: Simon & Schuster, 2003.

Nardo, Don. *Franklin D. Roosevelt: U.S. President.* Philadelphia: Chelsea House, 1995.

Phillips, Anne. *The Franklin Delano Roosevelt Memorial.* New York: Children's Press, 2000.

Potts, Steve. *Franklin D. Roosevelt.* Mankato, MN: Capstone Press, 1996.

Schlesinger, Arthur M. Jr., ed. *The Election of 1932 and the Administration of Franklin D. Roosevelt.* Broomall, PA: Mason Crest Publishers, 2002.

Schuman, Michael. *Franklin D. Roosevelt: The Four-Term President.* Berkeley Heights, NJ: Enslow, 1996.

Watkins, T. H. *The Great Depression.* Boston: Little, Brown, 1993.

MORE ADVANCED READING

Alsop, Joseph. *FDR: A Centenary Remembrance.* New York: Viking Press, 1982.

Burns, James MacGregor. *Roosevelt: The Lion and the Fox.* New York: Harcourt Brace, 1956.

Freidel, Frank. *Franklin D. Roosevelt: A Rendezvous with Destiny.* Boston: Little, Brown, 1990.

Gies, Joseph. *Franklin D. Roosevelt: Portrait of a President.* Garden City, NY: Doubleday, 1971.

Goodwin, Doris Kearns. *No Ordinary Time.* New York: Simon & Schuster, 1994.

Jenkins, Roy. *Franklin Delano Roosevelt.* New York: Times Books, 2003.

Places to Visit

★ ★ ★ ★ ★

Roosevelt Campobello International Park
P.O. Box 129
Lubec, ME 04652
http://www.fdr.net/englishii/

Visit the Roosevelt summer homestead on Campobello Island in Canada, just across the border from northern Maine.

Franklin D. Roosevelt Presidential Library and Museum
4079 Albany Post Road
Hyde Park, NY 12538
http://www.fdrlibrary.marist.edu/

See the president's home, personal effects, collections, and presidential library.

The Little White House at Warm Springs, GA
401 Little White House Road
Georgia Highway 85 Alternate
Warm Springs, GA 31830
http://www.fdr-littlewhitehouse.org/

Roosevelt sought relief from his paralysis and spent vacations here; he died here in 1945.

Top Cottage
The Franklin and Eleanor Roosevelt Institute
4097 Albany Post Road
Hyde Park, NY 12538

See the president's personal retreat on the grounds of his Hyde Park estate.

USS *Potomac*
540 Water Street
Oakland, CA 94607

Visit the presidential yacht that Roosevelt used until the United States entered World War II.

The White House
1600 Pennsylvania Avenue NW
Washington, DC 20500
Visitors' Office: (202) 456-7041

Tour the Executive Mansion, where the Roosevelts lived from 1933 to 1945.

The Franklin Delano Roosevelt Memorial
Ohio Drive SW, between the Jefferson and Lincoln Memorials
Washington, DC 20024
Information: (202) 426-6841
http://www.nps.gov/fdrm/home.htm

See the site divided into four "rooms" commemorating each of the president's four terms in office. There are sculptures of Franklin, Eleanor, and their dog Fala.

Online Sites of Interest

★ **Franklin D. Roosevelt Presidential Library and Museum**

http://www.fdrlibrary.marist.edu/

Offers information about the FDR Library, Museum, and special events.

★ **Roosevelt Campobello International Park**

http://www.info@fdr.net

Provides information about the island in Canada where the president's summer home was located.

★ **The New Deal Network**

http://newdeal.feri.org/

Provides many resources for the study of the 1930s and Franklin Roosevelt's presidency. Sponsored by the Franklin and Eleanor Roosevelt Institute.

★ **Internet Public Library, Presidents of the United States (IPL POTUS)**

http://www.ipl.org/div/potus/fdroosevelt.html

Excellent resource for personal, political, and historical materials about Franklin D. Roosevelt. It includes links to other useful Internet sites.

★ **The American Presidency**

http://gi.grolier.com/presidents/

Supplies biographies of the presidents at different reading levels from materials in Scholastic/Grolier encyclopedias.

★ **The White House**

http://www.whitehouse.gov/history/presidents

Provides information about the current president and vice president, a history of the Executive Mansion, virtual tours, biographies of U.S. presidents, and many other items of interest.

Table of Presidents

1. George Washington   **2. John Adams**   **3. Thomas Jefferson**   **4. James Madison**

	1. George Washington	2. John Adams	3. Thomas Jefferson	4. James Madison
Took office	Apr 30 1789	Mar 4 1797	Mar 4 1801	Mar 4 1809
Left office	Mar 3 1797	Mar 3 1801	Mar 3 1809	Mar 3 1817
Birthplace	Westmoreland Co, VA	Braintree, MA	Shadwell, VA	Port Conway, VA
Birth date	Feb 22 1732	Oct 20 1735	Apr 13 1743	Mar 16 1751
Death date	Dec 14 1799	July 4 1826	July 4 1826	June 28 1836

  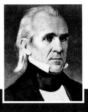 

9. William H. Harrison   **10. John Tyler**   **11. James K. Polk**   **12. Zachary Taylor**

	9. William H. Harrison	10. John Tyler	11. James K. Polk	12. Zachary Taylor
Took office	Mar 4 1841	Apr 6 1841	Mar 4 1845	Mar 5 1849
Left office	**Apr 4 1841•**	Mar 3 1845	Mar 3 1849	**July 9 1850•**
Birthplace	Berkeley, VA	Greenway, VA	Mecklenburg Co, NC	Barboursville, VA
Birth date	Feb 9 1773	Mar 29 1790	Nov 2 1795	Nov 24 1784
Death date	Apr 4 1841	Jan 18 1862	June 15 1849	July 9 1850

 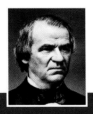   

17. Andrew Johnson   **18. Ulysses S. Grant**   **19. Rutherford B. Hayes**   **20. James A. Garfield**

	17. Andrew Johnson	18. Ulysses S. Grant	19. Rutherford B. Hayes	20. James A. Garfield
Took office	Apr 15 1865	Mar 4 1869	Mar 5 1877	Mar 4 1881
Left office	Mar 3 1869	Mar 3 1877	Mar 3 1881	**Sept 19 1881•**
Birthplace	Raleigh, NC	Point Pleasant, OH	Delaware, OH	Orange, OH
Birth date	Dec 29 1808	Apr 27 1822	Oct 4 1822	Nov 19 1831
Death date	July 31 1875	July 23 1885	Jan 17 1893	Sept 19 1881

	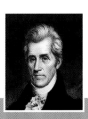		
5. James Monroe	**6. John Quincy Adams**	**7. Andrew Jackson**	**8. Martin Van Buren**
Mar 4 1817	Mar 4 1825	Mar 4 1829	Mar 4 1837
Mar 3 1825	Mar 3 1829	Mar 3 1837	Mar 3 1841
Westmoreland Co, VA	Braintree, MA	The Waxhaws, SC	Kinderhook, NY
Apr 28 1758	July 11 1767	Mar 15 1767	Dec 5 1782
July 4 1831	Feb 23 1848	June 8 1845	July 24 1862

13. Millard Fillmore	**14. Franklin Pierce**	**15. James Buchanan**	**16. Abraham Lincoln**
July 9 1850	Mar 4 1853	Mar 4 1857	Mar 4 1861
Mar 3 1853	Mar 3 1857	Mar 3 1861	**Apr 15 1865•**
Locke Township, NY	Hillsborough, NH	Cove Gap, PA	Hardin Co, KY
Jan 7 1800	Nov 23 1804	Apr 23 1791	Feb 12 1809
Mar 8 1874	Oct 8 1869	June 1 1868	Apr 15 1865

21. Chester A. Arthur	**22. Grover Cleveland**	**23. Benjamin Harrison**	**24. Grover Cleveland**
Sept 19 1881	Mar 4 1885	Mar 4 1889	Mar 4 1893
Mar 3 1885	Mar 3 1889	Mar 3 1893	Mar 3 1897
Fairfield, VT	Caldwell, NJ	North Bend, OH	Caldwell, NJ
Oct 5 1829	Mar 18 1837	Aug 20 1833	Mar 18 1837
Nov 18 1886	June 24 1908	Mar 13 1901	June 24 1908

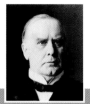

	25. William McKinley	26. Theodore Roosevelt	27. William H. Taft	28. Woodrow Wilson
Took office	Mar 4 1897	Sept 14 1901	Mar 4 1909	Mar 4 1913
Left office	**Sept 14 1901•**	Mar 3 1909	Mar 3 1913	Mar 3 1921
Birthplace	Niles, OH	New York, NY	Cincinnati, OH	Staunton, VA
Birth date	Jan 29 1843	Oct 27 1858	Sept 15 1857	Dec 28 1856
Death date	Sept 14 1901	Jan 6 1919	Mar 8 1930	Feb 3 1924

	33. Harry S. Truman	34. Dwight D. Eisenhower	35. John F. Kennedy	36. Lyndon B. Johnson
Took office	Apr 12 1945	Jan 20 1953	Jan 20 1961	Nov 22 1963
Left office	Jan 20 1953	Jan 20 1961	**Nov 22 1963•**	Jan 20 1969
Birthplace	Lamar, MO	Denison, TX	Brookline, MA	Johnson City, TX
Birth date	May 8 1884	Oct 14 1890	May 29 1917	Aug 27 1908
Death date	Dec 26 1972	Mar 28 1969	Nov 22 1963	Jan 22 1973

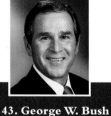

	41. George Bush	42. Bill Clinton	43. George W. Bush
Took office	Jan 20 1989	Jan 20 1993	Jan 20 2001
Left office	Jan 20 1993	Jan 20 2001	—
Birthplace	Milton, MA	Hope, AR	New Haven, CT
Birth date	June 12 1924	Aug 19 1946	July 6 1946
Death date	—	—	

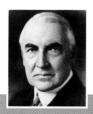

29. Warren G. Harding	30. Calvin Coolidge	31. Herbert Hoover	32. Franklin D. Roosevelt
Mar 4 1921	Aug 2 1923	Mar 4 1929	Mar 4 1933
Aug 2 1923•	Mar 3 1929	Mar 3 1933	**Apr 12 1945•**
Blooming Grove, OH	Plymouth, VT	West Branch, IA	Hyde Park, NY
Nov 21 1865	July 4 1872	Aug 10 1874	Jan 30 1882
Aug 2 1923	Jan 5 1933	Oct 20 1964	Apr 12 1945

37. Richard M. Nixon	38. Gerald R. Ford	39. Jimmy Carter	40. Ronald Reagan
Jan 20 1969	Aug 9 1974	Jan 20 1977	Jan 20 1981
Aug 9 1974★	Jan 20 1977	Jan 20 1981	Jan 20 1989
Yorba Linda, CA	Omaha, NE	Plains, GA	Tampico, IL
Jan 9 1913	July 14 1913	Oct 1 1924	Feb 6 1911
Apr 22 1994	——	——	June 5 2004

• Indicates the president died while in office.

★ Richard Nixon resigned before his term expired.

Index

Page numbers in *italics* indicate illustrations.

About the Author

Barbara Silberdick Feinberg graduated with honors from Wellesley College, where she was elected to Phi Beta Kappa and received the Woodrow Wilson Prize for an Essay in Modern Politics. She holds a Ph.D. in political science from Yale University. Among her more recent works are *Watergate: Scandal in the White House, American Political Scandals Past and Present, The National Government, State Governments, Local Governments, Words in the News: A Student's Dictionary of American Government and Politics, Harry S. Truman, John Marshall: The Great Chief Justice, Electing the President, The Cabinet, Hiroshima and Nagasaki, Black Tuesday: The Stock Market Crash of 1929, Term Limits for Congress, The Constitutional Amendments, Next in Line: The American Vice Presidency, Patricia Ryan Nixon, Elizabeth Wallace Truman, Edith Kermit Carow Roosevelt, America's First Ladies: Changing Expectations, General Douglas MacArthur: An American Hero, The Dictionary of the U.S. Constitution, The Changing White House, Abraham Lincoln and the Gettysburg Address: Four Score and More, The Articles of Confederation, The First Constitution of the United States, John McCain: Serving His Country, Joseph I. Lieberman: Keeping the Faith, Eleanor Roosevelt: A Very Special First Lady, John Adams*, and *Woodrow Wilson*. She has also written *Marx and Marxism, The Constitution: Yesterday, Today, and Tomorrow*, and *Franklin Roosevelt: Gallant President* and contributed entries to *The Young Reader's Companion to American History*.

Mrs. Feinberg is a native New Yorker and the mother of two sons, Jeremy and Douglas.